Reading for Pleasure and Reading Circles for Adult Emergent Readers

For Eva Muñoz: I love you so much.

Reading for Pleasure and Reading Circles for Adult Emergent Readers

Insights in Adult Learning

Sam Duncan

niace

promoting adult learning

Published by the National Institute of Adult Continuing Education
(England and Wales)
21 De Montfort Street
Leicester LE1 7GE

Company registration no. 2603322
Charity registration no. 1002775

The National Institute of Adult Continuing Education (NIACE) is an independent
charity which promotes adult learning across England and Wales. Through its
research, development, publications, events, outreach and advocacy activity,
NIACE works to improve the quality and breadth of opportunities available for
all adults so they can benefit from learning throughout their lives.

www.niace.org.uk

For details of all our publications, visit http://shop.niace.org.uk

Cataloguing in Publications Data
A CIP record for this title is available from the British Library

978-1-86201-823-5 (Print)
978-1-86201-824-2 (PDF)
978-1-86201-825-9 (ePub)
978-1-86201-827-3 (Kindle)

All websites referenced in this book were correct and accessible at the time of
going to press.

The views expressed in this publication are not necessarily endorsed by the
publisher.

Printed in the UK by Marston Book Services, Abingdon
Designed and typeset by Book Production Services, London

Contents

Foreword

I can't remember not being able to read. Reading is my comfort, my pleasure and my hobby. Reading makes me think, laugh and cry, and gives me a powerful sense of being connected to the world. I know that I'm lucky. I know that not everyone feels the way I do. My dad likes books and reading now, but couldn't read properly until he braved adult literacy classes when he was 29. At that time he learnt enough to write shift reports and that was all he needed. It wasn't until years later that he discovered the joys of reading for pleasure, and now we love to chat about books in our own reading circle. He enjoys recommending books to his friends. 'I never thought,' he said to me recently, 'that I was the sort of person who would be able to read books, let alone talk about them.'

Reading becomes richer – and more pleasurable – when you talk about it. One of things I most enjoy about my role as Project Director for Quick Reads is having the opportunity to visit facilitated reading groups for adult emergent readers. Reading can bring people together like nothing else can, and reading circles provide so much more than the opportunity to practise a skill.

A reading circle provides peer support. Whether they are helping each other with unfamiliar words or gaining fellow feeling from knowing they are not alone, talking about books with other readers gives people a sense of confidence and identity. A reading circle can enable individuals to join a community of readers for whom reading for pleasure grows and grows.

I am honoured to write the foreword to this book because I strongly believe that reading circles play a vital role in bringing the pleasure of reading to as wide an audience as possible, and particularly to adult emergent readers. Ideally, reading circles should be a core part of literacy development.

I'd like to leave you with two of my favourite quotes from our Quick Reads evaluation.

'I felt like I had climbed a mountain. I was so proud because it was the first proper book I'd read.'

'I never thought I'd be able to go to the reading group but now I sit and discuss books like I was born to it.'

Those two quotes sum up for me the joy that there is in both reading books and talking about books, and how privileged I feel that it is my work to strive to enable and empower more people to experience that sense of satisfaction.

Cathy Rentzenbrink

Project Director, Quick Reads

Introduction

I don't know who invented reading, but it's lovely.

(Anon)

This is a book about two reading practices: reading for pleasure and reading circles. It is about what each of these practices involve and the meanings they carry. It is also about how these two practices intersect: how reading circles are forms of reading for pleasure and how reading for pleasure nearly always involves some kind of the sharing or reciprocity characteristic of reading circles. Most of all, though, this is a book about reading for pleasure and reading circles for 'adult emergent readers' – a label which begs the question, who *are* adult emergent readers and what is emerging?

This book aims to share ideas about reading circles and reading for pleasure to see what we can learn from what has already been done and written, to share insights from recent research projects, and to listen to what members of reading circles have to say. It will create a distinction between two types of reading circle. The first type I am calling 'self-run' – those established and run by their members, like so many groups which meet on a regular basis in homes, cafés and bars around the world. The second are those set up by organisations or individuals on behalf of their members; for example, groups in libraries organised and run by librarians or groups in colleges set up by teachers. These are reading circles set up and managed by someone who is not a member of the group in the same way as the others. I am calling these 'facilitated' reading circles.

The distinction is important because this book is primarily for those facilitating, or planning to facilitate, 'facilitated' reading circles in different contexts. However, it is also for adult literacy teachers and for those supporting adult literacy development in prisons, libraries, workplaces and community centres who may want to use reading for pleasure and/or a reading circle approach either occasionally or regularly within teaching sessions. I hope this book will be of interest to anyone involved in first or second language reading development (including those working in English language teaching and English as a Second Language provision) and collaborative models of adult education. Finally, it is most certainly for anyone who has ever been a member of either type of reading circle, plans to start a reading circle, or who has ever sat down to 'read for pleasure'.

This book aims to examine how reading for pleasure and reading circles can serve adult emergent readers in particular but, in order to do so, it needs to explore what reading for pleasure and reading circles involve much more broadly. We will therefore keep moving from a tighter focus on the needs of adult emergent readers to a wider view of reading for pleasure and reading circles, and back again.

1

Context

Who or what are adult emergent readers?

I am using the term 'adult emergent readers' to refer to adults who see themselves as newer or beginner readers – adults who feel they want or need to develop their reading. These may be people who see themselves as 'non-readers' because they feel they cannot read. They may be able to read some pieces of text but not others. They may not feel confident that they fully understand what they are reading, or they may feel that they cannot read 'at all' (though others may disagree). 'Adult emergent readers' may also see themselves as 'non-readers' because they do not, rather than cannot, read. They may not read because they do not have the time, the confidence, or the inclination. They may actually read a lot every day but not consider this reading. 'Adult emergent readers' may feel that they are 'not the sort of people who can read like everyone else', or they may simply want to read 'better', 'more' or more widely.

The term 'adult emergent readers' is used to refer to those who lack confidence reading in any language. It is not normally used to describe those who are confident reading in one language and are now developing their reading, along with wider language development, in another language. This is how I am using the term, though certainly some adults trying to read in a new language, particularly using a previously unfamiliar script, may feel themselves to be 'emergent readers' in this new language, despite their confidence when reading their first or other languages.

I have been writing 'they' but the pronoun 'we' would actually be more appropriate. If you do not consider yourself an adult emergent reader, then you can be sure that someone close to you does.

The *emergent* part of the label is also a way of acknowledging that what happens when someone learns to read or develops their reading is a complex process of *becoming*, involving a tightly interwoven bundle of practices, skills and confidences and, crucially, that this process remains largely unknown or mysterious. Throughout this short book, it would be useful for us all – writer and readers alike – to keep one question in the front of our minds: *What exactly is emerging in adult emergent readers and how does it relate to reading for pleasure and reading circles?*

How do adults learn to read or develop their reading?

Here are four statements about reading:

1 *There is one right way to teach reading.*

2 *Universal schooling means universal literacy: where school is available, everyone learns to read at school.*

3 *If our schools and wider social provision did their jobs right, no one would need to develop their reading as adults.*

4 *You learn to read as a child, your reading development process finishes in your late teens and as an adult you are simply 'using' a fully-formed and finite set of reading skills (a bit like you use your adult teeth).*

I don't agree with any of these. I don't believe there is one right way to teach reading. There may be more and less effective methods for different people in different contexts, and there is certainly such a thing as 'better' and 'worse' teaching in a classroom situation, but there is no *one right way* to teach reading. Children and adults have been learning to read using an extraordinary array of different methods for centuries.

Nor do I believe that universal schooling means universal literacy. Not everyone is able to attend school regularly, not everyone who attends is equally included in learning (for reasons both within and outside the control of teachers) and not everyone needs the same amount of teaching or support. This means that we will always need opportunities for adults to develop their reading, not only for the reasons suggested above, but also because we all have different desires – and timescales – for reading development. Perhaps most importantly, we *all* develop our reading throughout our lives, because our needs and practices change, and technologies, genres, work and social norms change. We learn from each other constantly.

For hundreds of years both children and adults have learnt to read using many different methods and in as many different contexts: sitting with friends or neighbours with a prayer book or newspaper; following along as someone else reads; chanting letters, syllables and words; meeting in mutual improvement societies; or walking with a friend, matching words and pictures on shop signs. The history of how people have learnt to read is a story of a multiplicity of practices, approaches, techniques, texts, motivations and contexts (family, work, worship, prison, military, to name just a few). It is a story of children *and* adults, ordinary people and 'experts,' and it is a story of persistence and change.

INSPIRATIONS

- In the 17th century, a young man called Adam Martindale learnt to read with a beginner's book of words and prayers and the help of his sister's eager suitor.

- Early 20th century men and women learnt to read in 'Moonlight Schools' in rural Kentucky. These were adult schools which only ran on moonlit nights when there was enough light for people to find their way. Students started by learning to write their own names by tracing the shapes of the letters with their fingers or carving them onto thick paper.

- During the Second World War, British soldiers were taught to read using comics, football score sheets and racing results.

- Marie grew up in a village in Portugal in the first half of the 20th century. She learnt to read with her three sisters, reading illicit books from her grandmother's secret cabinet.

- Joseph Maylett was one of ten children of a farm worker in 18th century England. He never went to school and worked from a young age. When he was four, he was taught to read by his grandmother, using picture books.

- Pat went to school in the late 20th century, but struggled with reading for decades before learning to read with the help of actor friends and dozens of scripts after a discovered vocation as a stage actor.

See Houston (2002), Monoghan (2005) and Vincent (1989) in **Further reading** for more stories.

Adult learning

The 'Inspirations' stories tell us something about adult education more broadly. Adult education is often discussed in three categories. *Formal* learning occurs within official institutions, and usually with accreditation and some kind of social weight or recognition (for example, a two-year course to gain a catering qualification). *Non-formal* learning involves planned teaching, but without accreditation (for example, an Ethiopian cookery class in a church hall every Wednesday evening for two months). Finally, *informal* learning is a term used to describe the learning we do without planning it as learning or without learning being the primary aim of the activity (for example, I learnt to bake an apple pie from baking with my aunt). The lines between these are blurred and there is some variation in usage, but the important point is extent of the spectrum, from the learning that happens in large institutions with assessment and accreditation to the learning that happens when we are concentrating on something else.

For as long as people have read, adults have learnt to read in formal, informal and non-formal contexts. Much of this learning has been the result of what could be considered reading for pleasure – that reading we do simply for the joy of it; reading for its own sake. Much of this learning has also been in what could be considered reading circles – groups of people gathering to read together or to talk about what they have already read.

2
Background theory

Reading for pleasure

INSPIRATIONS

Why do people read?

I read to escape.
I read to travel.
I read to stretch my mind.
I read for the challenge.
I read to learn more, to learn all the things I never learnt at school.
I read for the fun of it!
I read to hear the voices of people long gone.
I read to find peace.
I read for company.
I read to pass the time.
I read because it makes me smile.
I read because it makes me think.
I read for the chance to stand in another person's shoes.
I read because it helps me understand my own life better.
I read because now I can.

What is reading for pleasure?

A pedagogic label

One answer to the question 'What is reading for pleasure?' is that it is a phrase used within educational settings to describe a *purpose* of reading: reading which is to a greater or lesser extent voluntary, marked by reader choice, of a text of interest to the reader, usually narrative (and often, but not always, fiction). It usually denotes an individual engaged in silent activity and, in the classroom, it sometimes indicates that reading will not be followed by related work or assignments.

Reading for pleasure is not, therefore, primarily defined by text type (though fiction or other narrative texts are characteristic), or even by whether the reading ends up actually being pleasurable or enjoyable, but rather by the original purpose of the reading. Reading for pleasure is not reading done for work, study or life administration purposes but rather *reading for its own sake*: reading because you want to, because it *pleases* you. Crucially, it is a term used within the contexts of educational research, policy and practice to describe the kind of reading which it is imagined happens 'naturally' outside of these settings, in the world of 'leisure'. The paradox is that reading for pleasure is not a term used in everyday life to talk about reading of this kind. We do not say 'I'm going to bed to read for pleasure' or 'I read for pleasure on the bus'. We would just say 'I'm going to bed to read' or 'I read on the bus', the lack of a stated purpose clearly indicating that the reading is for personal 'pleasure' purposes. The phrase 'reading for pleasure' therefore conjures a meeting – clash, even – of contexts: education and the everyday, or research and the personal or familial. It highlights the chasm between the unspoken 'taken for granted-ness' of leisure reading to those for whom it is a 'native' or habitual social practice, and the strangeness and mystery of this practice to its outsiders.

What pleasure?

The second way to answer the question 'What is reading for pleasure?' is to focus on the slippery word 'pleasure'.

What kinds of pleasures can reading bring? Answers from the literature can be grouped under five headings:

- pleasures of entertainment and escape;
- pleasures of cognitive work and narrative creation;
- pleasures of emotional stimulation: empathy, catharsis and intersubjectivity;
- pleasures of ethical contemplation: the 'should and could' of reading;
- pleasures of companionship.

These answers are considered in more detail below.

Pleasures of entertainment and escape

Reading narrative texts, particularly fiction, is often claimed to offer a form of entertainment which allows one to *master*, or gain control over time. This could mean to 'pass the time' on journeys or in prison, or to escape a particularly difficult present time in one's life. It could be a way to 'carve out' personal, private or quiet time amidst chaos or pressure. This may be the first thing that comes to mind when one hears the phrase 'reading for pleasure'. However, this escape from – or power over – time relies on the other pleasures listed below.

Pleasures of cognitive 'work' and narrative creation

Writing of drama (so, spectatorship rather than reading), Aristotle famously discussed two key literary pleasures: the pleasure of imitation and the pleasure of working out the imitations of others; the cognitive work of processing a text, of making sense of literature. Writing of the literary reading process and literary reader response and reception, theorists such as Wolfgang Iser and Stanley Fish (see **Further reading**) similarly emphasised the pleasures of the active, interpretive nature of reading, as the reader fills gaps left by ambiguous vocabulary or syntax and interprets spaces between sentences. The reader is undertaking complex cognitive work through interpreting, adjusting and creating. Similarly, both narrative theorists and psychologists interested in text-level reading have explored how, with each new paragraph or page, the reader constructs and reconstructs a 'story' as meaning is built, revised, assessed, rejected or adapted and rebuilt. Members of a reading circle I worked with stressed just how enjoyable these acts of 'brainwork', 'puzzling' and 'building' are. These are pleasures of intellectual or cognitive stimulation and creative satisfaction.

Pleasures of emotional stimulation: Empathy, catharsis and intersubjectivity

Reading narrative text (again, especially – but not exclusively – fiction) is frequently reported as being *emotionally* stimulating. For adult emergent readers there are two key elements to this stimulation: emotions which come from the act of reading itself (such as happiness at being able to read and understand a text, or unhappiness produced by difficulties with reading) and emotions which are felt as a result of plot or character developments (such as feeling happy when something wonderful happens to a character, or experiencing sadness when a character meets misfortune). The latter involves the emotional experience of empathy – but something more happens, otherwise why would we ever want to read a sad story? When we read novels we experience emotion in empathy with fictional characters, we develop our abilities to empathise *and* we enjoy practising this skill, meaning that even the experience of feeling sadness in empathy is enjoyable (Lisa Zunshine develops this argument in *Why We Read Fiction*; see **Further reading** for details).

Telling a slightly different story, Aristotle's notion of catharsis is usually interpreted to suggest that watching drama stimulates us to experience a range of emotions (terror and horror as well as joy) but that this stimulation is in itself inherently pleasurable because it purges us of the anxiety we hold at our potential for these emotions (see *Poetics* in **Further reading**). Yet another angle is taken by literary theorists borrowing from psychoanalysis, analysing how the novel reader takes on the subjectivity – the 'I' position – of the narrator and/or characters within the narrative to become someone else for a glorious while. When I read Murakami's *Dance, Dance, Dance*, I become his unnamed protagonist, both feeling his emotions and feeling a kind of joy at leaving my old tired subjectivity behind, if only for a few hours at a time.

Pleasures of ethical contemplation: The could and should of reading

Reading, particularly novel reading, has been damned as a 'silly mindless activity for silly minds'. At the same time, the pleasures of reading have been argued to be the product of absolutely 'serious' matters: political and ethical contemplation born from the perspective of seeing through other people's eyes. Literary theorists and philosophers have argued that novel reading allows one to observe the morality of action and consequence; to examine how one's actions touch others, and what this means for how we should behave. The novelist John Irving (see *Trying to Save Piggy Sneed* in **Further reading**) writes of the importance of the novelist exploring good and bad actions, creating what *could* have happened and therefore provoking analysis of the relationship between the 'could' and the 'should.' Alberto Manguel writes of the ethical and spiritual importance of the *possibilities* that reading helps us see:

> Books may not change our suffering, books may not protect us from evil, books may not tell us what is good or what is beautiful, and they will certainly not shield us from the common fate of the grave. But books grant us myriad possibilities, the possibility of illumination. (from *The Library at Night*, see **Further reading**)

Pleasures of companionship

Reading can connect us to other lives, emotions and possibilities. It can keep us company. It offers us what E. M. Forster calls the 'solace' we get from the lives we read about (see *Aspects of the Novel* in **Further reading**), it offers voices from across time and space and the companionship of other readers (such as in reading circles) and what writer and teacher Daniel Pennac calls the companionship of reading itself: '*We read because we know we're alone. Reading offers a kind of companionship that takes no one's place, but that no one can replace either*'. (From *The Rights of the Reader*, see **Further reading**.)

The obscurity and complexity of the term 'reading for pleasure'

The pleasures of reading for pleasure have therefore been identified in both academic and artistic discourses as pleasures of entertainment and escape; of cognitive work and narrative activity; of emotional stimulation, empathy, catharsis and intersubjectivity; of ethical contemplation; and of companionship. These are varied and complex joys – and of unambiguous value. The word 'pleasure' itself, however, *is* ambiguous. It often connotes sensual pleasure or appetite and frequently carries shades of indolence, or at least a lack of 'seriousness' or attention to 'things that matter'. The word 'pleasure' is therefore not an obvious signal for the potentially intellectual, political, educative pleasures outlined above. This means that the full nature and value of the reading practices referred to by the label 'reading for pleasure' is hidden from those who are not already 'in the know'.

What do we read for pleasure?

Personal choice is crucial to the definition of reading for pleasure. Anything that I choose to read for my own enjoyment is 'for pleasure'. Text type (a novel, a play, a newspaper, a cookbook) is therefore not the primary factor in whether something can be classified as an act of reading for pleasure; it does not have to mean novels. Yet it is true that many people do choose to read novels, as well as biographies, autobiographies and histories, for pleasure. These are narrative texts with twists and turns, characters, profoundness, the kinds of texts that 'draw us in', move us, give us peace and stimulation, solitude and company. But it is important to remember that what people read for pleasure could be *anything* at all, including magazines, sports pages, graphic novels, cartoons, reference books on favourite subjects, letters and poetry.

How do we read for pleasure?

If we want to understand reading for pleasure, one important question is *how* we read for pleasure. We turn letters of the alphabet into sounds, words, meanings, emotion and enlightenment. Inky squiggles on a page or letters on a little flashing screen become smiles and tears through cognitive, educational, communicative, imaginative and emotional processes of connection. But *how…* in what manner? When you imagine someone reading for pleasure, what do you see? Do you picture a person curled up under a blanket on a sofa? On a deckchair? In bed? Sitting? Lying? Standing? On a bus or train? Are their lips moving or still? Do you hear the words? Or did you picture someone reading to a huddled group of captivated listeners? Someone belting out from a stage? A father reading to a child? Someone reading to their sisters as they sit sewing? One lover reading to another? Did you imagine a crumpled paperback, a crisp hardback, a poster on the underground, a computer, a phone, a mural?

Reading for pleasure is very often an individual and silent practice and this is certainly our dominant cultural image. Yet it can also be a very loud and collective practice: a performance, an exchange, a communication. To complicate things further, individual reading for pleasure is not always silent. Think of medieval monks reading individually but aloud, if at a whisper, side by side, or a 21st century teenager reading song lyrics aloud from a smartphone. Nor is communal reading for pleasure always aloud. Picture a busy train carriage full of people with their heads in books. Like most reading practices, reading for pleasure is hugely varied. We read alone, in groups, in pairs, in families, silently, whispering and shouting.

Reading circles

One very popular and long-standing form of reading for pleasure incorporates silent *and* spoken, individual *and* communal reading: reading circles.

What are reading circles?

Book clubs, literature circles, reading circles, reading groups – the terms are varied and the practices even more so. Forms of reading circle have been around for as long as people have been reading. We probably each have an idea of what a reading circle is, even if we have a sense that practices vary.

Which of these are reading circles? Why or why not?

- *The Kalamazoo Ladies' Library Association of 19th century Kalamazoo, Michigan, USA, met once a month to discuss their chosen books, listen to lectures on a range of topics chosen by its members and plan participation in local politics.*

- *Neighbours meet every evening during Ramadan at one of their homes to read through the Koran. They listen to and correct each other's reading.*

- *In 16th, 17th and 18th century Germany, young, unmarried women gathered in spinning circles, or* Spinnstube, *to spin, read and talk.*

- *Six women in late 20th century Chicago meet twice a month in one of their homes. They eat dinner together, talk about their book and discuss their families. They also talk about who they are and who they want to be.*

- *Early Christians in Anglo-Saxon England came together to read the Bible, supporting each other's reading, interpretation and understanding.*

- *In some 21st century New York hotels, professional readers are available to read to guests in their rooms.*

- *Five sisters in 19th century North America formed their own literature club in their aunt's bedroom. They read novels to learn the things that their brothers learnt at school.*

- *English teachers in many Australian secondary schools ask pupils to sit in a circle and discuss a book, sometimes (but not always) following questions set by the teacher. The groups 'self-manage' with pupils taking turns to lead the discussion.*

- *A book club meets in a library once a month. Its members are adults learning English. They read a novel together, talking about the meanings of particular words, looking at grammatical structures and discussing the political/social issues which arise.*

- *Cuban cigar factory 'lectors' are employed to read novels and newspapers to the workers as they roll cigars.*

- *Six women in contemporary London meet every month to learn about science. A scientist is paid to attend and provide the science expertise, but the women choose the topic and prepare questions to kick off the session. They learn through discussion.*

Have you identified any that you feel are absolutely *not* reading circles? Or any that you feel most certainly are? Comparing our ideas would probably lead to a long discussion, in the course of which we may talk about purposes, turn-taking, reciprocity and power relations. Our discussion may lead to us agreeing certain criteria for reading circles.

We may agree that:

1 *Reading circles involve a written text or texts.* Whether text is read elsewhere and then discussed in the circle, or whether it is read within the circle gathering, aloud or silently, or whether there is one text or several, for something to be considered a reading circle, there has to be text.

2 *Reading circles involve turn taking.* A parent or carer reading to a child is not a reading circle, neither is one person reading aloud to a group of eager or not-so-eager listeners. A reading circle involves participating members taking turns to talk or read.

3 *Reading circles are non-hierarchical.* Even if different members take control sometimes, or members have certain specific responsibilities (for choosing a book, for buying cakes or keeping records), there is there is no permanent and overall leader.

4 *Reading circles are collaborative and involve peer teaching and learning.* Members learn from the texts and from each other.

5 Perhaps most fundamentally, *reading circles are based on discussion.* This could include discussion of the text and the personal or political themes that the text stimulates.

What do we know about reading circles?

We can learn about reading circles from our own personal experience as members of reading circles, but we can also read about reading circles. There are guides *for* reading circles (such as Jenny Hartley's *The Reading Group Book*, 2001 or *The Book Club Bible*, 2007; see **Further reading**) and there are novels and films *about* reading circles (such as *The Jane Austen Book Club*, a wonderful, funny book and a film). These can tell us what different reading circles have enjoyed reading, they can tell us why some people join reading circles – to pass the time, to make new friends, or simply to try out different types of books – and they can give us an idea of what actually happens in reading circles (arguments about politics or character motivation, tea drinking, sighs, laughs and exchanged glances?).

In addition, there are four bodies of academic research into reading circles. Research into reading circles used in contemporary school English classes tells us that reading circles can develop pupils' reading comprehension, learner autonomy and social skills. Research in English language teaching argues that reading circles can develop fluency in speaking and listening, reading and writing, and lead to vocabulary expansion. Research into reading circles in adult literacy education tells us that adults can develop their reading skills and practices, can teach and learn from each other, can develop their 'reading identities' as people who can and do read, and can develop speaking and listening skills as the reading circle provides a strong 'drive to speak' for those usually less confident in speaking. Ethnography and social history suggests that people have been gathering to read in circles for as long as we have been reading, including medieval holy men and women, 16th century French villagers, rural working men in 19th century New Zealand, pioneer women crossing the American West and undocumented hundreds of thousands seeking education, human contact and political organisation.

What is the appeal of reading circles?

Educational research, social history, ethnography and anecdotes suggest that the appeal of reading circles is as varied as their members. Some people join to develop their literacy or to broaden their general education. Some join to get to know their local communities or to create alternative communities. Some join for support with mental health issues. Some join because they want to read a wider range of texts, for new stimulation, for the challenge, the company or the opportunity to get out of the house. Some join to talk to people who are not their work-mates or family members, to talk about things other than spreadsheets, the economy or nappy rash. Many join for the chance to talk about the things they *really* want to talk about – what matters to them.

3
Getting started: Planning and setting up a reading circle

Models to think about when setting up a reading circle

A reading circle is a communal reading practice centred around written texts, involves turn-taking, is non-hierarchical and collaborative and creates peer teaching and learning opportunities through the central – absolutely vital – role of discussion. These characteristics provide the general shape of what we understand by a reading circle. And yet every circle is different. In the introduction, I placed reading circles in two main categories, those 'self-run' groups set up by their members, and 'facilitated' circles set up on behalf of the members and managed by someone external to the group, such as a librarian, a teacher or a union learning representative. This is certainly one major way in which reading circles can differ. There is, though, far more diversity than this. The examples that follow are drawn from a range of reading circles, not only those for adult emergent readers.

Diversity in reading circles

Reading circles are different sizes

Some have three members, some 12. I have never come across a reading circle with more than 12 regularly attending

members, and only two groups with three. This says something about the optimal number of people for a discussion-
based group, so that everyone gets the chance to contribute,
experience a range of views and also feel a degree of security
or intimacy. The vast majority of reading circles seem to have
between five and eight members, with six members attending
most meetings. Reading circles will grow and shrink.

Reading circles differ in where they happen

Living rooms, kitchens, cafés, church halls, libraries, prison
libraries, union learning centres, bus depot canteens – reading
circles take place in different locations and these locations can
make a difference in terms of how relaxed members feel, how
well they can focus and/or what they actually do together; for
example, whether members have anything to eat together or
not. Reading circles can change how someone feels about a
space. Members of a library-based reading circle I spoke with
explained that now they feel more like the library is 'for us'.

Reading circles differ in when and for how long they meet

Monthly? Fortnightly? Weekly? For an hour? A whole after-
noon? Different arrangements work for different groups. Less
confident readers or newer groups may prefer to meet more
frequently than once a month. Longer standing groups with
more secure membership may meet less frequently, perhaps
a few times a year, and still find this works for them. Some
groups meet for one hour, others for longer and some just
start and then see where it takes them. This has to do with
where and when they meet (demands on spaces and sched-
ules) on what else they do (do they have a drink or something

to eat?) and of course on the commitments and preferences of individual members.

Reading circles differ in the length of time they have been running, in how they started, in how long they will last and in their turnover of members

Some have been running for decades; others are brand new. This makes a big difference to what reading circles do and how often they meet. Circles start in different ways and for different reasons: some start as 'facilitated' groups and end up as 'self-run'. Some 'self-run' groups are started on the initiative of one person, others start as off-shoots of circles which have become too large and others still seem to spring into being through the serendipity of a series of events. *The Jane Austen Book Club* (see **Further reading**) started when one woman's husband leaves her, another's dog dies and a third women cries at the lost opportunity of a bad Jane Austen film adaptation. Members come and go, or come and stay.

Reading circles differ in the diversity of their members

A great many reading circles are single sex. Elizabeth Long's studies of Texan women's groups (see **further Reading**) suggest that, for some woman, the idea of a single-sex circle appeals because there are now very few other single-sex social gatherings and sometimes it is just nice to meet up with only women. There are also all-male groups, though anecdote would suggest far fewer. Some groups are composed of members of the same nationality (for example, a group of Japanese men in Cardiff), of one sexual orientation (for example, lesbian groups), some are composed of all of the same occupation (for example, all doctors or all accountants), some are fans of one particular genre (for example, science fiction or biography) and a great many reading circles are composed of people who all live within the same area or neighbourhood. These factors unite members of particular reading circles, just as age or educational background may unit members of others, but of course even within this uniting context (science fiction fans, doctors, or people who live in Catford), there are many ways that members are different – think of how different the women in a local women's group could be. Just as the 'uniting factors' may help members feel more secure to start with, the diversity is an important part of how any reading circle works, as members share their different perspectives and experiences. It fuels discussions and drives peer learning (see 'How we learn: An adult way of learning?').

Reading circles differ in the languages they use and the way they use them

A particularly interesting aspect of this diversity is language use. Unsurprisingly, many reading circles use the majority language of their local communities, whether that's English, Urdu or Spanish. Other circles are united by their use of a language which is not spoken by many others in their region – a reading circle in Germany, for example, composed of Welsh speakers. Some reading circles are composed entirely of those learning a new language; for example, a group of English, Australian and Canadian women in Bristol who read and discuss books in Italian as a way to develop their Italian. But here we have to stop and remember that reading circles involve both spoken and written language. Many reading circles read and discuss in one and the same language and others use one language for their discussion but read books written in another. I visited a reading circle of French women living in Leeds. They usually read novels written in English, but discuss them in their native French. There are rumours that a reading circle in Glasgow reads books written in a different language every month.

Reading circles differ in the texts they read

Many reading circles read fiction and almost as many read biography, history and autobiography. A few read epic poems. Some circles read, perform or discuss shorter texts such as magazine articles, poems, songs or recipes. Some read plays or screenplays and then perform the play, see the play or watch the film, and some read texts written by their members. Yet, for reading circles aimed at adult emergent readers, the question of texts is more complex (see **Building in sustainability**). Will members want to read the same range of books as anyone else? Or would texts specifically created for less confident readers work better – such as books published by Gatehouse, New Leaf, Quick Reads or Open Door? What is more supportive? What is most encouraging and motivating? And what is available? The Reading Agency has developed a website for participants in the Six Book Challenge, which supports less confident readers in their choice of books and gives them the opportunity to recommend books to others (see **Resources**).

The above is based on the assumption that everyone in the circle reads the same text and, while this is the dominant model, many circles involve each member reading a different text and then coming together to talk about them. A reading circle used to meet in a university building in central London. Its members were all from Ecuador. Their aim was to educate each other in political science and talk about the political movements important to each of them. They each read a different history/politics book every month and presented it to each other, summarising key points and recommending (or not) that others read it.

Reading circles differ in how they choose their texts

How do reading circles choose what to read? In some circles, members take turns to choose; other circles work from suggestions, taking turns or a vote. For some groups this is a very organised procedure, possibly planned a year in advance; for others it's more haphazard or simply led by availability.

Reading circles differ in the pace they read their books

Some groups read one book between meetings. They decide on a book at the end of one meeting, each member reads it in the time between meetings then the group discusses it at the following meeting. This is a familiar model, but not all groups work this way. Some groups like to meet to talk while they are still in the middle of a book, particularly if it's a very long book. Reading circles for adult emergent readers may want to take several months or more to read one book in a slower and more supported way.

Reading circles differ in what they do together

Reading circles are very different in how they spend their communal time. A significant difference is whether they read aloud together (either extracts of what they have already read at home, or reading 'ahead' together) or whether they prefer to do all their reading alone, coming together to talk about what they have read. Reading aloud can appeal if members want to enjoy the sound of the text, get feedback on their reading, or just practise reading aloud. Both less and more confident readers are often particularly interested in talking about *what has happened* in the book; to check if they have understood it 'right'; to affirm or challenge their own interpretations and for the joy of discussing characters and themes. Many also talk about what they like or dislike about the book, or about characters or events within the book. Beyond reading aloud and talking about the book, reading circles often spend their communal time talking about their own lives, eating and drinking and enjoying each other's company.

Reading circles differ in what members do between meetings

How much reading circle members read between meetings varies greatly, depending on confidence, time and preferences. In some circles, individual members write reviews or essays to read out or exchange in their meetings. In others, members practise reading aloud their favourite passages, ready to perform them and discuss them with the group.

Reading circles are different in their aims

Perhaps most importantly, reading circles have different aims, as groups and as collections of individuals. Some are built on an explicit longer term aim ('to develop our reading skills', or 'to develop our Italian language') but, for many, their only explicit aim is to read and discuss a book. Individual reading circle members, however, all have aims, implicit and explicit: to expand my reading, to get out of the house, to meet new people, to get to know my new neighbourhood, as a gentle way back into education – and many more. An important – and immensely valuable – characteristic of reading circles is the way in which one circle can usually satisfy all of these aims.

What do people actually talk about in reading circles?

Reading circle members talk about what words and sentences mean and what they found easy or hard, enjoyable or frustrating about the reading process. They talk through their interpretations of characters, events and themes and relate these to the characters, events and themes in their real lives. The best way to find out what reading circles talk about is to join or visit one yourself.

Here are some extracts from tapes of a reading circle discussing the novel *Passenger* by Billy Cowie. Names have been changed.

Rom: *And where is he from?*
Steff: *I think he's Scottish.*
Rom: *Does it say?*
Safia: *No, no it didn't.*
Andrea: *He lives somewhere in London, near Covent Garden.*
[....]
Steff: *How would you feel if you were Milan after the news leak?*
Maria: *Put yourself in his position –*
Rom: *Emotionally – it's hard –*
Safia: *He can't understand what's going on and then there are people chasing him.*
[...]
Safia: *What does she mean – palms forward?*
Andrea: *Like this* [demonstrates].
[...]
Andrea: *Why did Milan start smoking again?*
Rom: *Because his sister loves – she likes the nicotine.*
Steff: *How does she know –*

Rom: *Through the blood, through the blood –*

Maria: *So she's feeling it.*

Andrea: *He's smoking again because she loves it.*

Rom: *Karen doesn't like it though. She doesn't approve – because of the kisses –*

Safia: *She doesn't smoke.*

Steff: *It stinks – stinky breath – that's the kind of thing she would say –*

Rom: *I had a girlfriend who said that kissing me was like kissing an ashtray – that was awful – that was hurtful.*

[...]

Andrea: *Did Milan gain anything from this at all?*

Maria: *Yeah, I think he did. As we said in the beginning, he was a selfish young man and do things for himself and don't care but when he discovered his sister he became very caring –*

Steff: *Responsible –*

Maria: *Responsible.*

(See Duncan, 2012 in **Further reading** for a fuller discussion of this particular reading circle.)

What does a facilitator do?

For what we are calling 'facilitated' reading circles, the facilitator may well have been the person who set up the reading circle in the first place, thinking through the different options explored at the start of this chapter. The facilitator may choose the first book or may help the group choose, perhaps guiding their decisions. The facilitator may take control of logistics, like tea, coffee and biscuits (a pretty important part of proceedings according to one reading circle member: 'The tea and biscuits make it feel like somewhere you can breathe easy'). The facilitator may also take the lead in the first few meetings, welcoming people, getting the conversation going and, crucially, *modelling* the kind of ways one can talk about a book.

A facilitator may ask questions like this to generate or reju-venate discussion:

What stood out for you?
What did you think?
So, what was that all about?
Who do you think are the most important characters?
Tell me about him/her/them.
How did reading this make you feel?
What was going on in Chapter Two?
Did you come across any words you hadn't seen before?
Did anything really surprise you?
Why do you think X did that?
What would you do if you were X?
What do you think will happen next?
Did you enjoy reading it? What made it enjoyable/not enjoyable?

A facilitator may also encourage reading circle members to ask each other questions and should be on the look-out for members who may be quiet but actually keen to contribute ('Sam, what do you think?'). A facilitator's participation may become ever more marginal, moving towards a time when the reading circle members do not need the facilitator present and will 'self-run', or the facilitator may remain as a regular member of the group, providing stability and a constant point of reference as other members come and go.

Either way, the facilitator is there to support the group in self-managing as non-hierarchically as possible. A facilitator is not a teacher. Though some reading circles may have explicit literacy or language aims, and some facilitators may also be adult literacy or English for Speakers of Other

Languages (ESOL) teachers, the role of facilitator is not to teach literacy or ESOL, but to enable a peer-learning experience. Some of those who choose to join facilitated reading circles to develop their literacy do so precisely because they want to work with their peers and require a 'helper' not an expert teacher.

4
Teaching and learning

Literacy development

There are obvious problems with making claims about reading for pleasure and reading circles and the development of literacy skills. How are literacy skills defined and how are they to be measured? And even if measurement can satisfactorily demonstrate an advance in skills, how can anyone be sure that it is the reading for pleasure/reading circle that has had this effect, rather than all the other factors in each of our lives? But this doesn't mean researchers haven't tried. As noted earlier, research on the use of reading circles in secondary school English education has identified gains in reading comprehension and critical reading. English as a Foreign Language research in 'extensive reading' has argued that reading large amounts of self-selected narrative texts can develop reading fluency, vocabulary acquisition and writing skills.

Small-scale qualitative research into adult literacy development (see, for example, Kendall, 2008; Duncan, 2009; and Clarke, 2013 in **Further reading**) makes three main points about reading for pleasure, reading circles and adult literacy development. Firstly, it tells us that for most people, the best way to improve their reading is simply to *read as much as possible*. As one adult emergent reader explains, 'Read, read,

read! […] The more you practise the better you get at it, and that's the way it is.' The personal choice aspect of reading for pleasure means that readers are motivated and engaged in their reading. This will usually mean that they will read more, therefore getting more reading practice to improve their reading, from the word-level skills of whole word recognition and phonic decoding to the more interpretive aspects of sentence and text-level reading.

Secondly, and perhaps more surprisingly, adult literacy learners have reported that they feel that the memorable characters or events in true and fictional stories can help them remember particular words (both how to decode them and what they mean) by providing 'hooks' for the memory. One woman explained how the short book she was reading was so interesting to her that it helped her remember how to decode certain words, such as 'rice' and 'pudding.' She explained that she can now read these words when she comes across them anywhere, because 'When you read stories, and you find out a word, you don't forget because you remember the story'. Additionally, most narrative texts involve a degree of repetition of key items of vocabulary which provides further reinforcement to help readers remember these words. The word 'tumour', for example, keeps coming up in the novel *Passenger*. In this way, reading for pleasure can help with word-level reading skills in particular.

Finally, communal reading for pleasure, such as through reading circles, provides opportunities to *make visible*, *model* and *scaffold* text-level interpretive reading skills which are hidden in individual, silent reading. When reading circle members discuss a text – the meanings that are emerging, the characters' motivations and so on – they are interpreting the text together. This means that the interpretive processes which are often completely internal, hidden in individual silent reading for pleasure, become external and audible. In this way, reading circles model an interpretive process which is often obscure to newer or less confident readers: *What do we think about this character? Is she right to be angry or is she being unfair? And on what basis do we make our decision? What determines what's possible or not as an interpretation?* In addition, reading circles provide what we could call *scaffolding* for these interpretive skills, as more confident members provide support for those less confident, by saying more initially, or asking more questions.

I have been writing about reading *skills*; for example, the skill of being able to decode a written word, or the skill of being able to interpret a meaning expressed in sentences and paragraphs. I have also been writing about *practices*, of the things we do, such as reading in circles, reading alone, or reading because we want to read. It can be hard to separate skills from practices: is reading a novel a *practice* or a *skill*? Or both? The work of Steve Reder (see **Further reading**) reminds us how closely skills and practices are connected when we think about literacy development. Often the literacy 'gains' produced by participating in a literacy class or reading circle are the product of changes to literacy *practices*. The literacy class encourages its members to try out new literacy practices – for example, read the newspaper – and these practices, sustained over time, lead to developments in literacy skills.

We could additionally see this as a cycle involving another factor – what I have previously called 'reading identity', or how someone sees themselves in relation to reading. Starting a new literacy practice, such as joining a reading circle, can produce a shift in someone's reading identity; for example, from being someone who 'never reads' to being someone who 'can sit and talk about a book'. This new reading identity opens up new reading practices and these practices, over time, develop skills. This is not entirely unproblematic as a way of talking about reading as we are still left with questions about the nature of skills and their relationship to practices and reading identity, but it is nevertheless useful as a way of reminding ourselves how difficult it is to separate notions of skill and practice, and how crucial identity is, however they connect. Furthermore, thinking about skills, practices and 'reading identity' can be a helpful way to understand the role of a facilitator, as someone who isn't teaching literacy but is supporting people to develop their literacy by supporting practices and shifts in 'reading identity'.

Reading aloud

What is reading aloud?

We say 'reading aloud' rather than just 'reading,' and yet, outside of school settings, we rarely say 'reading silently'. This suggests that silent reading is now the 'norm,' or most common type of reading, while reading aloud is strange, note-worthy – the exception. It certainly wasn't always this way. Reading aloud has been the dominant form of reading over most of the world since writing systems were developed. Some believe that reading aloud only stopped being the dominant form when more people could read than couldn't (around the late 19th century in much of Europe). There is a famous story of the young Augustine arriving in Milan and being simply amazed to see Ambrose reading without moving his tongue or making any sounds. Augustine was used to rooms of men reading individually, but *aloud,* if quietly (see Manguel's *A History of Reading* in **Further reading**).

Today, many of us would be equally shocked to find a library full of individual readers uttering the words they were reading. Our current cultural 'norm' of individual, silent reading is strong. Yet it shouldn't be overestimated. Our lives are still full of reading aloud. We read aloud to children, in cafés when looking at menus with friends, in religious worship and, often, when trying to understand complex instructions. If you start looking, you will find many examples. Reading remains a practice which is both silent *and* aloud, individual *and* communal.

Some years ago I interviewed 35 adult literacy learners about reading, asking 'What are we doing when we read?'. As I had hoped, their responses taught me a great deal about reading. They taught me that we can understand or categorise reading aloud in two ways, that it is both a way to get better at reading (a *pedagogy* if you like) and a type of reading in its own right (a *practice*). As a reading development pedagogy, learners spoke of reading aloud alone at home as part of developing confidence with phonic decoding: 'It [reading aloud] helps you because you see the word and then you try to position your mouth to how the letters are written'. Others spoke of reading aloud in front of others in a class or with friends in order to get feedback: 'I like [reading] loudly because I am learning something... it's good that other people hear – if there is a mistake they can help'. Finally, and crucially, they pointed out how useful it can be to follow along in a written text as you hear someone reading aloud:

> *You know before, when we used to read in class, yeah, I used to pretend I was following, but I wasn't – but now I do follow it! I notice that it helps me a lot... when someone's reading it and you're following it, it helps – if you can't say that word, don't know what that word is and someone's reading it, and then it's "oh yeah yeah". That helps a lot.*

As a particular reading practice, the learners noted that reading aloud can be a very private practice, for example as part of religious worship: 'It's better to read it [a Holy Book] aloud because you feel the words, every word you read you feel the word... putting all of my mind and my heart in it'. In addition, they discussed reading aloud as a performance, whether to a group of adults or to one child: 'You have to push your voice out, and make every word perfect, so they can hear you and understand'. Finally, they spoke of the importance of hearing certain texts aloud, in order to be able to understand them better or differently: 'I like someone reading poems to me; I understand when someone is reading'. Margaret Atwood shares this belief in the importance of hearing certain texts read aloud and explores the importance of the ear appreciating short stories: 'I'm not arguing for the abolition of the eye, merely for the reinstatement of the voice, and for an appreciation of the way it carries the listener along with it' (see Atwood in **Further reading**).

Reading aloud, reading for pleasure and reading circles

Not all reading for pleasure involves reading aloud or listening to others read aloud, but much does. Lovers read to each other, parents to children, friends to each other, and some hotels even have readers that guests can hire. Certainly not all reading circles involve reading aloud, but some do. Reading circles for adult emergent readers in particular may find reading aloud useful for individual members to get:

a) feedback on their reading (*Is that right? Have I said it right? Is this the word I think it is?*);
b) help with decoding the words they are unsure of (*What is this word?*);

c) the chance to listen to others read aloud and therefore get valuable support with linking written words with spoken words;

d) the opportunity to practise the real life reading skill of reading aloud, which they may want and need in other areas of their lives.

Facilitators of reading circles for adult emergent readers may want to establish ground rules for 'jumping in' when someone is struggling to read a word; for example, how long would individuals like others to wait before helping them decode a word, who should help and how.

Other learning

What else do we learn?

Reading for pleasure additionally provides what could be called broader or wider learning opportunities through what the texts themselves teach us. This learning has several important elements. It is about learning specific pieces of information from the books we read, about trains and hospitals, religions and geography, specific times and places. It is also about learning about the lives of others, about learning to see through someone else's eyes. This is a way to understand other people, other situations and other points of view. This is the learning that comes from a move away from a single dominant perspective, allowing us to climb into others' shoes, gain a bit of vicarious experience and, in doing so, potentially understand our own roles better. Reading circles may amplify this aspect of reading for pleasure by providing the perspectives not only of those within the text one is reading, but of those within the reading circle.

Reading circles also offer additional learning as participants work together in a group. This includes discussion skills such as turn-taking and exchanging points of view; social skills such as welcoming others, exchanging greetings and putting others at their ease; and community participation. Members of a reading circle for adult emergent readers explained to me how important this aspect of their learning was to them. They emphasised the sense of 'achievement' that they felt at being able to successfully 'operate' as a member of a reading circle. They stressed that if you can sit with a group of people who are not family, work colleagues or old friends, and talk about a book (something you may have struggled to read), then you know you can cope in a range of situations, from job interviews to parent-teacher meetings: 'It is huge. It's achievement'.

How we learn: An adult way of learning?

I am arguing that reading for pleasure and reading circles are particularly *adult* ways of learning because they are driven by adult choice and direction. People select books that deal with themes which are of interest to them as adults; members of a reading circle will choose which of these themes to discuss, and then decide how to discuss them in order to produce a particularly adult and personally meaningful discussion about the book, these themes and the members' lives. Members of a facilitated reading circle for adult ESOL learners explained that they chose to join a reading circle rather than an ESOL class because they wanted to talk about 'adult things' in 'an adult way'. They read three novels over six months and in doing so talked about different political regimes, love, jealousy and raising children.

Reading circle members also *direct their reading circle work* in two clear ways. The first is what could be called, in educational terms, a *'negotiated syllabus'* – the group negotiates, more or less explicitly, what they want to do and how. For example, they discuss how much they want to read each month, which books to read and how long they want to spend on their discussions. Every member, ideally, has an input in these negotiations as the reading circle continuously adapts how it works. The second way that members of reading circles direct their work is in what I've called *'participant-led differentiation'.* This is the idea that even within a group situation everyone needs to do slightly different things (differentiation) according to *their own assessment* of their needs and interests. A reading circle member who wants to develop her spelling may copy out and practise ten words from the book every week, and therefore for her, the reading circle involves spelling practise. Another member may particularly want to develop his active vocabulary and another may want to practise her speaking and listening. In this way, reading circle participants provide themselves with differentiated learning.

Finally, reading circles can be considered particularly adult forms of teaching and learning because of the peer learning opportunities offered, via scaffolding and the 'mutual exchange of expertise'. The term 'scaffolding' is often used in education studies to mean a type of support given to a learner to allow them to develop particular skills. For example, if someone wants to learn how to structure a letter of complaint, a teacher may provide scaffolding with spelling (writing up a list of common words on the board, for example) so the learner doesn't need to worry about spelling while trying to concentrate on paragraphing. Reading circles, both facilitated and 'self-run,' involve a great deal of scaffolding. Members provide each other with scaffolding in the form of remembering what has happened in previous chapters (to help one person understand better what he/she is reading now), or reading aloud for each other (to help another person concentrate on text-level interpretation without having to focus on word-level reading).

This scaffolding is based, at least in part, on something we could call 'the mutual exchange of expertise'. Within any group of adults, there will be someone knows a lot about X and someone else who is really good at Y. Reading circles work as peer-learning opportunities precisely because this expertise is exchanged: 'I may need help with decoding but I can help you with the meanings of hospital-specific vocabulary', or 'I need help remembering what happened in the last chapter but I can tell you what a "thimble" is'. A facilitator can encourage and celebrate this exchange of expertise.

Links to other provision

Finally, we can think about how reading circles (and reading for pleasure more generally) relate to other forms of learning. Earlier we discussed how reading circles can be situated within formal provision, even within particular classes. In addition, reading circles can take place within colleges or community centres as extra activities for those taking scheduled classes. Reading circles are also held in libraries, union learning centres, workplaces and prisons; and they happen outside of any kind of organisational structure at all – under a tree, in a café, in someone's home. There are therefore a range of relationships between reading circles and other kinds of education. A reading circle could be a stepping stone leading to non-formal or formal education, or it could be *instead of* non-formal or formal education, preferred by someone who doesn't want to join a class or cannot commit that amount of time. A reading circle can also be alongside participation in educational provision, as a complement or supplement to what a class is providing. Facilitators need to be aware of these potential relationships, as well as of the educational desires of those in the circle. Those working in non-formal or formal educational should also try to be aware of the reading circles around them, which may appeal to their students.

5

Engagement:
Two case studies

The more groups I visit, the more convinced I am that, along with literacy and other learning, reading circle members are constantly *making connections*: with their fellow reading circle members, with their local communities, with characters and narrators in the books they read, and with local and global communities of readers. In making these connections, in these acts of engagement, members of reading circles seem to be expanding or exploring who they think they are, what they are capable of and what they think is important or valuable. Here are two case studies which may help to illustrate this point. Names have been changed.

ANNA

Anna has been a member of her reading circle for nine months. She joined after seeing a notice at her local library. She grew up in Greater London; she went to school but didn't like it and left without any qualifications. She says she 'could read a bit but not very well'. She sometimes used to read with her grandfather, who was 'a brilliant reader', and she got a little better in her early twenties, but still thought of herself as someone who 'can't really read properly' and so 'didn't really read'. She always had a job – mainly in local shops – until she had her first child seven years ago, when she was in her late twenties. She's got two children now, one seven and one five, and is a full-time mum. A few years ago, she started taking her children to events at the local library to encourage them to read and, in doing so, decided to try to develop her own reading. She thought about taking a course at her local college but didn't like the idea of a formal class and 'wasn't sure what would be right for me'.

When she saw the sign for a reading group in the library she really liked the idea. She had heard of groups before but they were always in the daytime and she couldn't do that because of the children. On the first day she arrived late and was too shy to ask where the group was, but she asked the librarian about it the week after and arranged to join the next month. When she started the first book she was nervous, unsure if she could finish it, but 'It was fine actually. I could read nearly all the words and ended up finishing it after just one week!' She was nervous before the first session, 'Wasn't sure what to expect, who would be there', but was pleasantly surprised to find five other women, 'really nice' and some of them 'very chatty'. As they started to talk, Anna soon found herself joining in and 'It's carried on from there... I read mainly when the kids are in bed. I look forward to it, to the reading and to the chats in the library'. She enjoys the social, local aspect:

It's good to meet people who live nearby and to have a reason to talk to them. I love talking but I'm not good at starting conversations. I'm a bit shy. It's good to have a focus to what you're going to talk about. Though sometimes we end up talking about different things, you know, war, love, kids, men, the government – it's all here!

Before she joined the group, Anna didn't read much:

Only what I had to – letters, bills, the odd magazine... I knew I could read, but never thought of picking up a book – or thought of it but something stopped me... Also, what do you choose? There are so many. How do you know what's good or not? Things like that stopped me.

She saw a 'good reader' as someone surrounded by bookshelves and able to talk about anything: 'I knew I wanted my kids to be good readers'. She likes how the reading circle 'forces' her to read more books and different kinds of books, 'things I'd never heard of'. She comes 'to be pushed to read more','to sit with others, to talk' and 'to keep learning. I learn so much from each book. It can be hard but we get there and then I know something new'. Anna thinks most people come to the group for the same reason. Some people, she thinks, really love the talking, while others want to be encouraged to read. She thinks some others in the group were probably not very confident readers when they started but they are 'getting there now'. Their group read mainly fiction, a mixture of Quick Reads (see **Resources**) and other novels. She likes the length of the Quick Reads but she also likes to read 'the great classics, the ones some people read at school. I want to have read those too'.

Being in the reading circle gives Anna

...a proper sense of achievement. I've done it – I've read this book, and that one and that one! And I talked about it, with the rest, held my own if you see what I mean... It makes me feel more educated. I mean, maybe it shouldn't

matter what you did at school, but I do want to feel like I can read and discuss something properly. I want to feel like I can explain it to my children, can help them, can show them... It's not easy reading a whole book, but when you've done it, you know you can do it again. You get better at reading each word and you get better at pulling it all together, you know?

Anna isn't looking for work right now but feels it will help her when she does because she is a more confident person and will feel more able to sit in an interview situation with several people facing her. She would recommend joining a reading circle for this reason, 'especially if someone's been out of work for a while – it would be a good way of getting used to dealing with other people again'. But she also recognises that reading circles are alien to a lot of people: 'If you hadn't joined a group, or hadn't seen one, witnessed one, you would have no idea what goes on, what we do, or why they should come'.

Anna stressed how much she enjoys her reading. She felt it was similar to watching films or TV in some ways ('You get hooked on the story', 'You want to know what's going to happen next', 'You care about the characters') but also different:

You have to concentrate more... You can't just sit back and wait for it to come to you... You have to put a lot of effort in, to read, to think, to imagine but then you get a lot out as well.

TOM

Tom is in his fifties. He joined his group about two years ago. He was talking to a librarian, asking her to recommend a book ('not too long, not too hard') and she told him about the group. He comes most months and always reads the books even if he doesn't come to the meetings. He likes history and biographies best. Tom grew up and went to school in another country and arrived in London to work when he was in his early twenties. He has some O-Levels. He never felt he was a bad reader, but knew that some people were 'much more educated and read more'. He has always worked, mainly manual jobs which 'don't need any reading so I never get much practice'. Before he joined the group, Tom read the newspapers. He used to watch people reading books on the bus and was 'amazed at how transfixed they were. So into it! So focused! I wanted to try it'.

Tom feels he has gained a lot from the reading circle:

> *I learnt a lot from each book. Facts, history, places, religions. I got all that. And talking about it you get even more. I have my ideas, and then when I tell them, someone else tells their ideas and I have to think again. Where do they get that? Did I miss that? What else did I miss? What else is there? Sometimes I read it again, the book, I read it again to see what else is in there.*

Tom really values the exchange of ideas. He also feels that his reading has improved: 'My reading is better, better meaning I can read more quickly and have more confidence that I have caught the right meaning'. Tom thinks that most people in the group come for the same four reasons: 'Social, the group, the talking, the tea and chat – we all love that', developing their reading skills, reading a wider range of books, exchanging ideas and learning from each other.

It has changed how I feel about myself as a reader. This is true. I know I can pick up any book, yes, I think any book, and give it a try, see how it goes. And I enjoy the reading.

Tom analysed what makes reading enjoyable, or pleasurable, for him:

It's the journey. You are on a journey, often to different places and times. You can go where you maybe never get the chance to go or maybe you go where you have been before and you remember – that is special... and it is full of emotion – maybe pain, maybe joy, maybe heartache – but you feel. It is healthy to feel so much, to think so much. Some may think it's not healthy but it is – good for the mind and soul.

Tom felt it was similar to watching a good film, the same emotion 'and suspense' but different in that: 'With books, you have so much more choice. There is so much. You could never read all the books in the world. Endless'. This idea of choice is important to Tom, that he is reading something he wants to read and in a way he wants to read it. It's 'something I'm doing for myself'.

6

Impact: Making a difference

What do we know so far?

We know that many members of both self-run and facilitated reading circles value their circles and feel that their reading circle work has had an impact on their personal, professional and family lives. We know this from qualitative research of the kind that created the case studies in the previous chapter. We can continue to collect these sorts of testimonies, talking to members and facilitators, observing and taking part in sessions.

How else can we measure or capture the impact of reading for pleasure and reading circles? This needs a lot of thought. This book is, in part, a call for future research and, perhaps first, for wider discussions about research agendas and methodology. Here are some questions we could start with:

What are the key messages we need to get 'out there' and who do we want to be listening?

How can we measure the literacy and wider language development produced by reading for pleasure and/or reading circles? How can we measure other changes to practices and confidences?

How can we measure the impact that reading for pleasure or a reading circle may have on the reading habits or attitudes of someone's children?

Can or should we measure community participation, enjoyment, inspiration or happiness?

Another way of looking at this is how you, as facilitators and members of reading circles, can measure impact. Here are some suggestions:

a) Ask the members of your circle what they think. Ask, ask and keep asking. Ask different questions and use different words. Get everyone thinking about the effect the reading circle has had on their lives, including their family and community interactions.

b) Watch what various members of your reading circle do over the months or years you are together. Look out for what changes or develops.

c) If you are a facilitator, talk to others in your organisation, and to those facilitating similar (or different) reading circles. Go back to the original aims for starting your reading circle and think about how well those aims have been achieved. Think about what else has come from your group.

d) If you are not already a member of a reading circle yourself, join one. Even if you join a 'self-run' group for confident readers, rather than a facilitated group for less confident readers, the experience will give you a different perspective and a stronger sense of the potential impact of reading circles, how they reach and shape different parts of our lives.

7
Building in sustainability

Reading circles are usually low on bureaucracy and high on 'real activity' and adaptability, which means they have in-built sustainability. This is why some groups have been running for 30+ years. There are, however, serious challenges to getting a reading circle started and keeping it going.

Getting the word out

Self-run groups usually operate by word of mouth, with an individual or small group starting them and then each member asking someone else to join, and so on. Facilitated groups are can be more challenging to get started, especially if the facilitator is not already in regular touch with those for whom the group is intended. For example, if I want to start a reading circle for adult emergent readers in my local library, I would probably want people living in the area who are not confident in their literacy to join. How do I know who they are? How do I get in touch with them? How do I spread the word? Are there community learning champions, outreach workers, youth workers, librarians, staff in schools and children's centres, members of faith communities or others with an overview of learning in the community who I could talk to? I could try putting up posters in the library and local area, but what should they say? Which words do I use? How much text is appropriate? I will need to think about where else to advertise and who else to talk to. I could work with local colleges, community learning settings, community groups and children's centres. I would hope that once one or two people come, they would tell others and so, gradually, our reading circle would establish itself.

Recently, I have spoken to facilitators in children's centres and other community learning centres who have 'spread the word' by holding coffee mornings where they talk through the idea and get as many different people thinking about it as possible, including those who may never have imagined they'd be interested in a reading circle. Overall, the biggest challenge when running a reading circle is getting it started and reaching those not actively seeking one.

Attendance

Irregular 'attendance' or participation can pose a challenge to any group. Because reading circles will usually, hopefully, feel like something non-compulsory, non-forced in a world of unpleasant obligations, they may be the first thing to get pushed to the side when life gets complicated and diaries overflow. However, this non-compulsory feeling is also part of the appeal of reading circles, and so members do come back when they can.

On a practical level, discussing the days and times of meetings and their frequency (not too often as to be inconvenient, not too distant as to break momentum...) with the group to find an arrangement that works best for most people is important, as is stressing that it is normal that not everyone can come to each session (so don't worry if you can't always come) and providing a way to keep in touch between meetings. I visited a reading circle based in a library that had a bulletin board where members could post ideas or leave notes for each other in between meetings. Speaking to another circle, I found that one member who could not attend every session would regularly send a friend to deliver her thoughts jotted on the back of an envelope. Many reading circles have a phone number or numbers that members can call if they cannot attend so that they feel 'in touch' and not inhibited about returning the next time.

Choosing the text

A reading circle needs a text (a book, usually) and what that text is, who chooses it and where it comes from is another potential challenge. Who chooses? How do you choose something that everyone will like? Is it important that everyone likes it? In a facilitated reading circle it may work best for the facilitator to choose the very first book, second-guessing what would work in terms of interests and literacy confidences, and then, once the group is established, to ask them to decide how to choose texts in the future. Other facilitators start with a general discussion about reading preferences and then get the circle to choose their first book. Availability of (multiple) copies needs to be a factor in choosing. The following are a few more points to bear in mind.

It is rarely possible to find books that everyone will like, all the time. It is not even necessarily desirable that everyone loves the book. Many members of 'self-run' reading circles say that they joined their circles to get some diversity or freshness into their reading, to take them away from their same, safe choices. To come across a book that some members of the circle do not like is not a bad thing, as long as you can generate a discussion about *why* they don't like it. Remember that not liking a book is not the same as not enjoying the reading circle discussions. Asking interesting questions, getting members to talk about what they do and don't like and why certain books do and don't appeal, and who would and wouldn't like them can make for an engaging discussion. Further, making sure you discuss the themes in the book more broadly, making sure those who are not so keen on the book are included and have plenty of opportunities to speak, can mean that the reading circle continues to be a pleasure even if the book isn't. It is important to remember that less confident readers may blame themselves if they are not enjoying a book and so may need to be reassured that it is fine to stop reading a book if it is not enjoyable; no one likes everything.

It is also crucial to think about literacy 'levels' or confidences when choosing a book. Years ago, when I did a CELTA teacher training course (teaching English to speakers of other languages), I came across a phrase that I will always remember: 'Grade the task not the text'. In an English as a Foreign Language context this meant that you can use any text with any group of learners, provided you change what you do with it: it is the task which needs to be adjusted according to language level, not (necessarily) the text. This is a useful reminder that you can actually use any 'level' text with any group of learners/readers, provided you change how you use it. *However,* certainly, if the aim is for everyone to read the whole book, this is going to be difficult if members of the group do not feel able to read more than a few words. In this case, it may be best to start with shorter books written specifically for, and often by, adult literacy learners, such as those published by Gatehouse and New Leaf (see **Resources**) or shorter, simpler texts on photocopied sheets. Not using 'real' books, may make it feel less like a reading circle for some members, but a) it is usually more motivating to tackle more manageable texts and b) many adult emergent readers find it extremely motivating to read books written by adults who have themselves struggled with their reading. Try out different texts and talk about what works and what doesn't.

Finally, many reading circles read poems and songs. Poems can be short and many extraordinarily beautiful poems are written using simple words and more straight-forward linguistic constructions. Many are easily available online and are from a range of cultures. Crucially, poems can work very well with groups of adult emergent readers because the actual words of many poems are relatively straightforward to decode and being faced with (for example) 20 words arranged on a sheet of paper can be less daunting than pages of continuous text, and yet the conceptual and philosophical difficulty of many poems is high, making them more interesting and motivating and absolutely 'adult'. Some poems can require less confidence in one's word and sentence level reading skills, while requiring a lifetime of adult experience to understand their deeper meanings. This can make them ideal for reading circles for adult emergent readers.

Mixed levels

Earlier, in the 'Teaching and learning' chapter I argued that reading circles can provide a great deal of participant-led differentiation and peer scaffolding, allowing people with different needs and strengths to work together effectively, teaching and learning from each other in a mutual exchange of expertise. This means that someone who is a bit less confident with one aspect of the reading process can get support for this from others, while in turn offering a different member support with something else. This often works well, but there are limits. If differences in reading experience or confidence, particularly around decoding, are too great, it can be hard to sustain everyone's interest and motivation.

Here is some advice from those who have facilitated or taken part in reading circles which catered for a wide range of literacy 'levels' or confidences:

- *Reading out loud can help. Some members of our group cannot read much, so they listen to others read and then join in the discussion. Some try to read it themselves at home with family afterwards, once they know what it is about. They say it makes it easier. We also limit the amount any one person can read aloud, so that if someone wants to read a lot, but struggles, the process is not frustrating for them or others.*

- *Listening to an audio version of the text before reading it, or even instead of reading it, can allow less confident readers to enjoy a book and contribute to the discussion.*

- *For us, our group is primarily a discussion group. We focus on the themes from the book and how they relate to our own life experiences. This means that everyone can feel engaged and involved, regardless of how much each of us is able to read (alone or together). Some people don't read the whole book, sometimes they just don't have time.*

- *We have really different literacy levels in our reading club, so we don't all try to read the same thing. We meet every two weeks and at the end of each session we choose a topic for the next meeting. Then everyone reads something on this topic. I [the facilitator] help some of them find things to read, others find their own. Then we come back together to tell each other what we've read and talk about what the texts had in common. For example, recently we looked at war writing. Two people read war novels (different ones), one person read a short piece of biographical writing I helped him find, one person read a longer war poem and one person read a much shorter poem (I helped with this). They each told each other about what they had read – which everyone loved – and then we had a long discussion about war.*

- *In my reading group, we are at different levels. I've been going for a few years and have been doing classes too so I'm one of the more confident ones. We each find something to read during the month and then tell each other about it. This is good because even if someone can't read much, they can choose something they can read, and when they listen to us all talking about our books, they get more ideas of what to read.*

Finally, remember that there are many different reading circles around, to suit different levels of reading confidence and other personal preferences. Facilitators should aim to be aware of as many different local reading circles as possible, to refer individuals onwards if it seems that a different group would suit someone better.

Maintaining interest

Reading circles, however they are set up, seem to come alive in a slightly mysterious way. They become entities greater than their individual members, formed by and constantly reforming those members. A multitude of different factors – including chance encounters, coincidences of timetables, serendipity of life and text, and group dynamics – mean that some groups really 'take off' while others don't, and some continue strong for years while others suddenly fade. It is hard to pinpoint why. 'Self-run' reading circles are, by nature, largely undocumented, rarely leaving a paper-trail and so it is extremely difficult to try to learn lessons from their successes or failures.

Facilitated groups are a little different in this respect, and there are lessons to be shared. The facilitator is very important; he/she can set the tone of the reading circle so that everyone feels respected, valued, listened to, safe and welcome. If a reading circle takes place within, for example, a workplace, or prison, or library, then it is also important how the group is positioned in relation to the whole organisation. Is it valued? Does it have a dedicated place to meet? Do members feel that the reading circle is *theirs* and a space where they can be something other than employees or prisoners or members of the public? Anecdotally, the most long-lasting reading circles, both self-run and facilitated, are those flexible enough to evolve with their members and contexts, to meet new and changing needs and challenges.

8

Where next?

We probably need more research studies, more evaluations of impact, more explorations of different types of reading circles and different models of reading for pleasure. Get involved. Try something and write about it, show it to someone else and take it from there. If you are a facilitator, you could visit other reading circles, see what they do and report back to your circle. You could also think about your own next steps. Are you interested in teaching? Would you consider training to be an adult literacy or ESOL teacher? If you are a member of a reading circle, you could consider joining or visiting another circle for more ideas, writing about your group, or becoming a facilitator of a facilitated reading circle.

All reading circle members and other readers are heading off into the unknown in terms of digital texts, electronic reading devices, use of social media, and the increased possibilities of interactive online reading communities developing. We will see where we end up!

9

Final thoughts

This book has been a discussion of reading for pleasure, reading circles and the potential needs of adult emergent readers. I have tried to outline what, why, where and when people read for pleasure; presented reading circles in their various manifestations; and explored what reading for pleasure and reading circles can, and do, offer adult emergent readers. I have argued that reading circles are both a 'real life' adult literacy *practice* and a potentially rich adult literacy *pedagogy*: that within reading circles, adults can teach and learn from each other, developing literacy alongside all sorts of other knowledge and skills. This does not mean that reading circles should be seen as a replacement for more formal adult literacy provision; far from it. We will always need adult literacy provision (in colleges, community centres, workplaces and prisons) to meet the needs of adults wishing to develop their literacy in a classroom or workshop environment.

But reading circles offer something different: a chance to read, think and talk in a collaborative, supportive setting. Both facilitated and self-run reading circles can support adults in their particular learning needs, just as they can provide company, inspiration, challenge and a community connection. Reading circles help us to remember that reading is a communal as well as an individual activity. We can read *to* each other and in the company *of* each other, but we can also truly read *with* each other, by forming interpretations in conversation with others and therefore carrying out text-level reading processes collaboratively.

The more I talk to people about their reading, and the more I read about reading, the stronger certain key messages become. Overall, it seems that we human beings simply really like stories; our minds are good at finding, grasping and creating stories. We tend to remember stories and those stories can help us remember other things, from words to facts to important moral lessons. Many of us like to read, as well as hear, stories – and when we do read stories, most of us really want to talk about what we have read. We seem to create and recreate our identities through the stories we hear, the stories we read and the ways that we talk about them. This goes some way to explaining the appeal of reading for pleasure and reading circles.

Some years ago, I think it was a particularly cold and lonely late December, I read something which expressed the appeal of reading for pleasure in a different way. It was part of Ludovico Ariosto's 15th century epic poem, *Orlando Furioso*. I'll try to tell the story as I remember it. In the midst of 1600 pages of tales of battles, romance and heroics, one scene stood out. Hero Orlando discovers that the woman he loves is with another man. He goes into a frenzy, destroying whole forests by plucking up the trees like dandelions with the superhuman strength of his fury. His friend Astolfo watches and quickly decides that there is only one solution: he flies on his horse to the moon to try to recover Orlando's lost wits (because 'whatever has been lost on earth is found upon the moon'). On the moon Astolfo sees everything that has ever been lost on earth, from 'the tears of lovers and their endless sighs' to 'vain projects none could ever realise', and 'unfulfilled desire, which occupies more room than all the rest and more expanse'. He finally finds a pile of 'tightly corked' little jars of wits, including 'a great part of his own' and 'the wits of those he thought had none'. He soon finds a jar labelled 'Orlando's wits' and brings it back down to earth. He gives it to Orlando and they carry on with their knightly adventures.

Flying to the moon, unbound by our earthly bodies, to rummage through the wits of others (horrors, seductive and repulsive, as well as beauties) – and some of our own we hadn't even realised we were missing – before returning to our own worlds, healed, transformed and longing to ride again. Isn't this what we are doing whenever we read for pleasure?

10
Glossary

Autobiography: The life story of an individual, written by that individual themselves. An autobiography is usually taken to be representative of true events.

Biography: A story of the life of a person, usually taken to be a representation of the truth.

Decoding: The reading skill of identifying a printed word (or part of a word) and turning that printed word (or part of a word) into a sound and/or meaning.

Differentiation: A term used in education studies; the idea that the teacher (or teaching and learning situation) takes into account different learners' interests, levels of confidence and previous experiences.

Facilitated reading circles: Reading circles established and managed by someone on behalf of the group, usually by someone in an official capacity (such as a librarian, teacher or union learning rep).

Fiction: In classification of texts, fiction refers to texts which are not claimed to be 'true' but rather are the product of the author's imagination. Novels and short stories are genres of fiction.

Formal education/learning: A way of classifying learning experiences, formal learning occurs within official institutions, usually with accreditation; for example, a GSCE English class at a further education college. See also **informal education/learning** and **non-formal education/learning**.

Informal education/learning: A way of classifying learning experiences, informal learning is usually understood to mean the learning that we do without planning it as learning; for example, learning to use the Paris metro system as part of living in Paris. See also **formal education/learning** and **non-formal education/learning**.

Narrative: Narrative can mean an account of a sequence of events, or the telling of that account, in spoken or written words or in pictures.

Non-formal education/learning: A way of classifying learning experiences, non-formal learning is usually understood to mean planned learning but without accreditation; for example, an adult yoga class without any form of accreditation or certification. See also **formal education/learning** and **informal education/learning**.

Novel: A book-length piece of prose fiction.

Participant-led differentiation: When individuals (such as members of reading circles) organise their own **differentiation** by adjusting what they do according to their needs and desires.

Reading circle (or book club, book group, literature circle, etc.): A group of people who gather to discuss, and sometimes read from, a written text. See page 43 for a full discussion.

Reading for pleasure: The reading that one does simply because one wants to. See Chapter Two for a full discussion.

Scaffolding: A term used in education studies; the idea that a teacher or other learners can provide 'support' for certain aspects of a task or learning activity, so that an individual can concentrate on other aspects of the task. See page 39 for a full discussion.

Self-run reading circles: Reading circles established and managed by their members.

11

Further reading

Ariosto, L. (1977) *Orlando Furioso, Vol. 2*, translated by B. Reynolds. Harmondsworth: Penguin Books.

Aristotle (1996) *Poetics,* translated by M. Heath. Harmondsworth: Penguin Books.

Atwood, M. (1989) 'Reading Blind: The Best American Short Stories 1989', in M. Atwood (Ed.), *Writing with Intent: Essays, Reviews, Personal Prose 1983-2005,* pp. 68–79. New York, NY: Carroll & Graf Publishers.

Clarke, G. (2013) 'Reading for pleasure: creating a virtuous circle', *Research and Practice in Adult Literacy*, 79, pp. 15–17.

Cowie, B. (2008) *Passenger.* London: Old Street Publishing.

Duncan, S. (2009) '"What are we doing when we read?" Adult literacy learners' perceptions of reading', *Research in Post-Compulsory Education,* 14(3), pp. 317–331.

Duncan, S. (2012) *Reading Circles, Novels and Adult Reading Development.* London: Continuum.

Fish, S. (1980) *Is there a text in this class? The authority of interpretive communities.* Cambridge, MA: Harvard University Press.

Forster, E. M. (1927) *Aspects of the Novel.* Harmondsworth: Penguin Books.

Fowler, K. J. (2004) *The Jane Austen Book Club.* London: Penguin Books.

Hartley, J. (2002) *The Reading Groups Book* (2002–2003 ed.). Oxford: Oxford University Press.

Houston, R. A. (2002) *Literacy in Early Modern Europe: Culture and Education 1500–1800.* London: Longman/Pearson Education.

Irving, J. (1993) *Trying to Save Piggy Snead.* London: Black Swan.

Iser, W. (1972) 'The reading process: A phenomenological approach', in D. Lodge (Ed.), *Modern Criticism and Theory.* London: Longman.

Kendall, A. (2008) '"Giving up" reading: Re-imagining reading with young adult readers', *Research and Practice in Adult Literacy,* 65, pp. 8–13.

Long, E. (2003) *Book Clubs: Women and the Uses of Reading in Everyday Life.* Chicago, IL: University of Chicago Press.

Manguel, A. (1996) *A History of Reading.* New York, NY: Viking.

Manguel, A. (2006) *The Library at Night*. London: Yale University Press.

Monaghan, E. J. (2005) *Learning to Read and Write in Colonial America*. Boston, MA: University of Massachusetts Press.

Murakami, H. (2002) *Dance, dance, dance,* translated A. Birnbaum. London: Vintage.

Pennac, D. (2006) *The Rights of the Reader*, translated by S. Hamp Adams. London: Walker Books.

Reder, S. (2009) 'Scaling up and moving in: Connecting social practices views to policies and programs in adult education', *Literacy and Numeracy Studies*, 16.2/17.1 (1), pp. 35–50.

The Jane Austen Book Club (2007) (Film) Directed by R. Swicord, USA: Mockingbird Pictures.

The Book Club Bible (2007) London: Michael O'Mara Books.

Vincent, D. (1989) *Literacy and Popular Culture: England 1750–1914*. Cambridge: Cambridge University Press.

Zunshine, L. (2006) *Why We Read Fiction: Theory of Mind and the Novel*. Columbus, OH: The Ohio State University Press.

12
Resources

This is a starting point, not an exhaustive list. There are other publishers and websites.

Gatehouse Books: www.gatehousebooks.co.uk

National Adult Literacy Database Library (Canada's Literacy and Essential Skills Network): http://library.nald.ca

New Leaf Books: www.newleafbooks.org.uk

Open Door books for less confident adult readers: www.newisland.ie/fictionopendoor

Oxford University Press Bookworms Reading Circles www.oup-bookworms.com/reading-circles.cfm

Quick Reads website, full of resources and ideas, including the 'Quick Reads reading group toolkit: www.quickreads.org.uk

Research and Practice in Adult Literacy: http://rapal.org.uk

The Reading Agency: reading groups for everyone, www.readingagency. org.uk/readinggroups

The Reading Agency: section on libraries, http://readingagency.org.uk/about/libraries.html

The Reading Agency: Six Book Challenge website, including database of titles, fact and fiction, from pre-Entry to Level 2 www.readingagency.org.uk/sixbookchallenge and www.readinga-gency.co.uk/findaread

Unionlearn: www.unionlearn.org.uk

See also your local library services.